Tim & Beverly LaHaye

Our Favorite Verse

ACCENT BOOKS
Denver, Colorado

Photographs by Shirley Brown (pages 4,9,13); Mary Nelson (pages 7,11,15,17,19,21).

ACCENT BOOKS

A division of Accent Publications, Inc.
12100 West Sixth Avenue
P.O. Box 15337
Denver, Colorado 80215

Library of Congress Catalog Card Number 86-70647

ISBN 0-89636-215-9

OUR FAVORITE VERSE

In the early days of our marrige we had an average relationship with occasional high mountains and sometimes low valleys. We met in college and married before graduation, and we were probably too young and immature to know why we did not have a better beginning.

College life was very demanding. We each carried a full load of studies while trying to develop a lasting marriage. Being a young bride, I wanted to create a cozy home environment in the simple three room apartment we had rented, and Tim was delighted as he accepted his first church as a week-end pastor.

Like most young married college students we also had financial problems that put added pressures on our lives. Tim would be in classes all day and study well into the night, but that did not keep him from taking an early morning paper route that he could deliver before sunrise. This brought in enough extra money to help pay our rent, but it left little time to build our marriage. School tuition was costly and neither of us had parents who could help pay for our schooling. Government aid was non-existent. I worked part time in a C.P.A. office and became an Avon lady plus held an assortment of other jobs to help cover our tuitions.

Tim's mother had raised him after his father's death. He was only ten and as the oldest of three children, he became his mother's confidante. She discussed the problems of her life with him and leaned on him as he carried the role of male advisor to their household. He really had no example set before him of the position that a husband and father should take. On the other hand, my father died when I was two years old and my mother remarried when I was four. My stepfather was a very strong man and filled the position of husband and stepfather with real authority. The fact that Tim had no father and I had a strong one created some differences in attitudes and responsibilities in our home.

We have recounted some of the obstacles in our early marriage not to give an excuse for our young, immature actions but more to explain what we needed to overcome.

- We were young and immature with selfish motives.
- We had college studies that took a great deal of time.
- We were learning to adjust to each other.
- We had financial pressures.
- We were pastoring our first church.
- We had part-time jobs.
- We came from different backgrounds on the man's role in the home.
- We carried family problems into our marriage.
- We had little time for just us.

But we adored each other and we both wanted to follow God's leading in our lives! Unfortunately, those first few years established some poor standards for us and it took many years of struggle to find the key for overcoming our common difficulties. However, we both came from families who had instilled into our values the conviction that marriage was a commitment for life. Yes, there would be problems, but you sought solutions not separation. So we stayed together and stuck it out. Even when we were at our worst, divorce was only a fleeting thought, quickly dismissed because we knew that somehow, someway we would find an answer.

Babies began to come into our household and changed the number from the "two of us" to the "four or five even six of us." We discovered that children do not resolve problems. They more often rearrange and add to your problems, especially if you have not learned how to cope with the ones you already have.

Not only had the size of our family grown, but the little things that had irritated us also grew. Our full time church was now taking more and more of Tim's time and attention. Financial pressures were always looming over us. It seemed like Tim's impatience and angry nature became worse and worse, and my worried, fearful disposition was destroying any confidence that we could build a happy marriage.

At that time it seemed like we were the only couple with such difficulties, but since then I have learned that many couples stagger under the weight of similar pressures. Some are able to ride the storm and live out

their lives on such a rocky foundation. Others have collapsed and ended the marriage through separation or divorce. But there is another group of people that have found the key to building a contented and happy marriage relationship. Tim and I are blessed and privileged to have found the secret.

Twelve years into our marriage with four children gathered around us and pastoring a growing church, it appeared on the surface like we had everything a couple could want. But we both longed for a better relationship with one another.

We had learned how to put on a front to cover our conflicts as we walked out the door of our home and to pick them up as we re-entered. It was amazing how you could remember just where you left off in a heated discussion and carry on as though there had been no interruption.

Up to that time we knew very little about the work of the Holy Spirit in the life of a Christian. Our church and educational backgrounds had said very little about the practical influence of the Holy Spirit in one's life. We had seen those who talked about it on Sunday, but during the week showed little evidence of the indwelling and transforming power of the Holy Spirit. That was not what we wanted.

Then I heard about a Sunday School Conference to be held during one week in June at Forest Home Conference Grounds in California. Tim was unable to attend so another friend and I decided to go. She worked in the Sunday School also and we were going to find new ways to teach and build our church's youth

work. But it turned out to be a conference that built our marriage and helped us.

Dr. John Hunter of Capernwray, England and Dr. Henry Brandt, a Christian psychologist, were the two speakers. One spoke about the victorious Christian life through the work of the Holy Spirit and the other speaker explained how the true filling of the Holy Spirit would affect every area of your life. It would change your attitudes, your actions and even build a deeper and more contented relationship with your husband. It wasn't by some magical, quick change, but by a growing understanding of how to cope with conflicts and misunderstandings. I heard for the first time how the filling of the Holy Spirit would help me to love others more fully—I needed that. I could have a peaceful heart—I needed that. I could experience an inner joy and I needed that. I had developed a habit of looking on the negative side of things and that did not produce joy.

As the speakers continued in their dynamic messages, it was as though they were speaking directly to me. I could have been the only one in that room because everyone else just seemed to fade away. More and more it became evident to me that many of my problems and our problems stemmed from my selfish attitudes. Not only did I relate most situations to how I would be affected, but I also had a selfish interest in my time, my love for others, my giving or sharing, my involvement and a critical attitude toward life in general.

When the last speaker shared how the filling of the Holy Spirit would cause one's life to bear the fruit of

the Spirit such as love, joy, peace, patience, kindness, goodness, faithfulness, gentleness and self-control, my heart longed for all those blessings in my life becaue I knew I lacked many of them. It became evident in those few minutes that I had been trying to put a marriage relationship together by myself, without the control and the power of the Holy Spirit in my life.

Meanwhile, Tim had been planning to drive up the mountain to meet me and take me home. I reached him by phone the day before he was to leave and encouraged him to come early to hear one of the speakers. He must have sensed my enthusiasm and change of heart, because he decided to arrive in time for the closing session.

This last message explained that even after the Holy Spirit was in control of your life, it was possible to grieve the Spirit by being angry or bitter. How could that speaker know that this was Tim's need? Once again it was as though that sermon had been directed at one of us, and this time at Tim. He squirmed and fumed, thinking that I had tipped off the speaker and then invited him to come for the shoot-out.

Tim had struggled with his angry heart for many years and finally had passed it off with a "that's just the way I am" attitude. In past years there had been several stormy days as he reacted to situations that "were not perfect" with an angry spirit. When he would show his anger at me, I would "clam up" and be silent. Silence became a way of retreating from reality for me until gradually it was simpler to have little communication between us.

As the meeting closed, though, Tim was broken-hearted over grieving the Holy Spirit and responded to the Scripture that calls anger and bitterness a sin. He asked the Lord to forgive him, and was totally repentant because he too longed for the fullness of joy and the abundant life that we were not experiencing. In the same conference, the same location and the same week, God dealt with us individually over our separate problems.

The Scripture verses that helped us separately and now together are Ephesians 5:18-21:

> **" ... be filled with the Spirit, speaking to one another in psalms and hymns and spiritual songs, singing and making melody with your heart to the Lord; always giving thanks for all things in the name of our Lord Jesus Christ to God, even the Father; and be subject to one another in the fear of Christ."**

We learned at that conference the importance of the Holy Spirit's indwelling us and allowing Him to transform our natures to be more Christ-like. And it could not be just a Sunday morning experience. It would be every day and in every circumstance.

In fact, after verse 18 says to be filled with the Spirit, the next three verses describe how life will be when you are controlled by the Spirit. First, you will have song or melody in your heart regardless of the problems facing you. Why? Because the problems are no longer yours alone, but are shared by the heavenly Father who cares for you. Secondly, you will be able to give thanks for all things by faith before you even know the end result. And last, your focus will no longer be on

yourself but on others. Because of the love given by the Holy Spirit, you will be able to lovingly serve others. When these principles are put into practice in the daily life of a married couple, their relationship will be transformed—and ours was truly changed.

It was not a quick healing but rather a gradual growing and building together. There were many times when we had to ask forgiveness of God and one another and go back to the basics, but at last we were growing together!

It has now been over twenty years since that conference and those difficulties are behind us. I cannot say they are forever gone, but as we walk together in the Spirit, we can expect God's blessing on us. I have watched my husband gradually change from an impatient, angry person to a gentle and kind individual who is filled with compassion for others. Some may say that it is maturity, but I believe the only answer to his dramatic change is the result of the indwelling Holy Spirit influencing his life day after day.

My life has changed as well. I know because the feelings of insecurity, selfishness and fear that I once had have been replaced with confidence, love for others and peace in my heart.

Our marriage has been greatly strengthened and enriched as we have learned to walk in the Spirit and to let the Holy Spirit have complete control in our lives. That experience caused our marriage to change from just commitment to each other to becoming real companions and best friends. We do recognize, however, that if we failed to obey the Word of God and

His principles for righteous living, we would quickly revert back to our old, natural ways. The happiness and joy we experience today can be related to how much of God's Word we are obeying and putting into our daily lives. We consider Ephesians 5:18-21 our favorite verses because without them our marriage may not have been saved.

Because of the effect and change the Holy Spirit has brought into our lives, we not only have a wonderful relationship, but God has allowed us to have a shared ministry through our Family Seminars. We have been privileged to see many couples, who were enduring mediocre marriages, begin to fall in love all over again when they allow the Holy Spirit to take control. After all, the first fruit of the Spirit is love and Tim and I have learned how to truly love each other.